The Magnifying

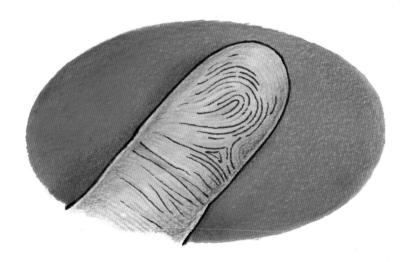

Written by Karen Anderson
Illustrated by Peter Paul Bajer

Look through the magnifying glass.

What can you see?

2

A spider leg.

3

Look through the magnifying glass.
What can you see?

4

A feather.

Look through the magnifying glass.
What can you see?

A leaf.

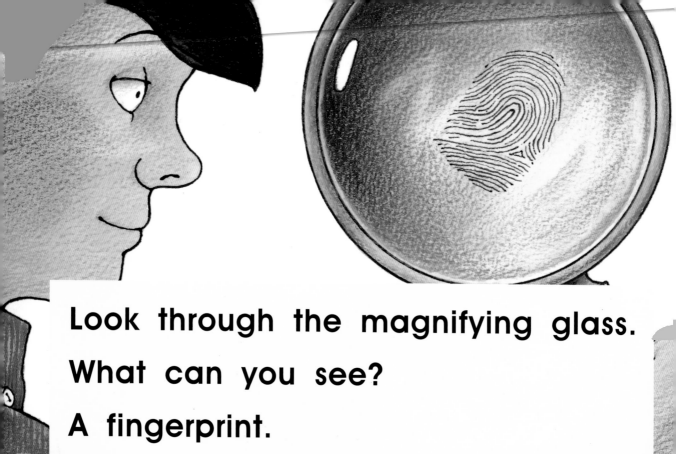

Look through the magnifying glass.
What can you see?
A fingerprint.